Live Canon
2020 Anthology

First Published in 2020
By Live Canon Ltd
www.livecanon.co.uk

978-1-909703-84-1

The right of the poets published in this anthology to be identified as the authors of their work has been asserted by them in accordance with Section 77 of the Copyright, Design and Patents Act 1988.

A CIP catalogue record for this book is available from the British Library.

Live Canon
2020 Anthology

*The poems in this anthology were longlisted for the
2020 Live Canon International Poetry Prize*

Contents

Pariah
Akshayaa Chittibabu

"Of all the world's wonders, which is the most wonderful?
That no man, though he sees others dying all around him,
believes that he himself will die."   The Bhagavad Gita

When the plague came   America once again
became the world's   most wonderful place
the globe glittered then burned   like storm kissing sun ray
my Father sat on the throne   and watched the rain bow
then break

        those days   I sat and watched and everything loomed

I had often wondered   in my youngest brownhood
what it must feel   like to be holy
to be revered   the highest ranking
untouchable

the Boy I could have loved worked in the hospital
if the plague was a prayer   He told me the confessions tore
flesh from husk   skinned pears with jagged finger nail
held them prickled   til they wrinkled
crisp white   then brown then browner then brownest
the plague   took Boy and wiled him to pariah

        those days   I think we were all briefly holy

                I can't do this   Boy said one night
                    Oh I said   *This? or... this?*
                I don't know   we both slept

9

with our phones by our faces
scrubbed all of it with soap in the morning

as Death abounded   I asked Him once
    to take me   alone
    even in the plague   God refused me

    those days   we reminded
    ourselves   of ourselves
    over and   over and
    over and   over
    that killed us the most

as Death abounded   I craved everything
warm bread mostly   fingers in my mouth
fingers wherever they'd fit
white wine and whole milk and being loved

made do peeling galas and pink ladies into
    soft curling ribbons of speckled fleshed red
let the cores rot   let the skins rot
    squashed rot between fingers
until there was no white left
    brown then browner then brownest

when I stopped telling where I began and the apples ended
my skin   finally   burned from fever

i watched the plague flirt   and asked it to kiss me
    it slept with me and left

    those days   I scrubbed myself anytime I wanted to feel something

when eyes blurred with salt   I peeled oranges
first pierce the rind   hook jagged finger nail
tear orange from white

      those days   all I did was pierce and hook and
                                       tear

each day praying   I ask anything that listens
      to never make me god
begging that that would be enough
bring fruit to tooth and bite
      isn't it wonderful to be alive

West/East
April Yee

My eyes are the hammered edge
of a Chinatown butcher's cleaver,
heavy and heaved with momentum,
not sharp. There's enough sharpness
in sheared bottles, wires embroidered
with barbs, paid bills that slip
inside the flesh. I heave my eyes
on discards, cleaving past
from present: Who touched this can,
and can it buy my lunch? My butcher
heaves his cleaver through
a duck's shiny body, and I see
the X-ray of its bones, perfect whites
circling congealed purple cores.
The rice: free, my butcher's Buddha
plea. I swallow slowly, seeing
with my tongue for paddy stones
that seek to crack my teeth.

I picked one time a book,
heavy with large font:
The Geography of Thought.
A man inside theorised
mankind's mind cleaved
in the age of the ancient Greeks,
each fisherman hauling his solo
catch while Chinese strewed
rice across collective fields.
West sees the thing; East sees
the place the thing sits in.
I can see I am now West:
sifting, sorting, seeing the trash,
and not the street the trash sits in.
Someone saw this book as trash.
Were I East, I'd be the rice,
the duck, and the butcher,
whole in every grain.

Paul Stephenson

See how the boy sits, slim on a rotten wooden chair that's just about standing. There, he just about sits at the end of a long narrow garden of hard clay soil, the lawn of scrappy grass that gently climbs. From the end he surveys the rear of the red-bricked terraced house he lives in. He sits by day with distance and sky and often now, when the wooden chair permits, sits on into the night.

There are people in the house, his house, people in the kitchen whose back door opens out onto steps leading down to a yard and a long narrow garden. He sits, boy-like, there at the end of the garden, his garden, in the company of foxgloves that love the dim light and damp, thrive in the partial shade of the neighbour's mature trees, sycamores in full leaf on either side, closing in.

Bodies are moving within the backdoor's frame, people talking in the house, but the foxgloves are quiet in the garden as he sits on the rotten wooden chair he's carried to the end, precariously, and sometimes a fox. Between the low slat fences and tall stems of pink and purple hoods, and the bees, behind a glossy screen of shrubs, the tower of summer lilac at the end of the garden, he sits.

With a feint-ruled notebook and pen to hand, a can of warm cider by his feet, at the very far end of a long narrow lawned garden the boy writes, writes words that are legible only to him. He writes as he sits, sitting out the summer with himself, by himself, just about him. The people, all the people, he opened the door when the doorbell rang and, one after another, they let themselves in.

Nausicaa
Nora Nadjarian

I handed him   the sea-steeped sheet   I'd been washing
        and as he covered himself
with it and   it clung to his body like skin
        I knew I'd done what a sculptor
does with marble   making him my own
        His salt-stung eyes and smile   searched
my face   This is how the story began

        with the sea as backdrop   surging.

Under my closed lids   is another story
        All night the dampness   of his long
hair washed with olive oil   I can taste   Wear this I say
        wear this   and kiss him

        my lips like a fish   drinking him in.

I gave him food and wine
        let him sleep in the guest bed I stripped   on the day
he set sail   That sheet   I carried once more   to the shore
        immersed it in loss
did what a sculptor does with marble   made it one
        with my naked body

        Did you tell her   about me?

        The sea took you   as far back as I can remember.

Design of Deaf-Aid and Conference Amplifiers with Corrected Characteristics, August 1938
Lisa Kelly

The Post Office Engineering Department is considering
my request. I told them I want to take part in conferences.
As an officer of the Engineer-in-Chief's Office, I want to get on,
want to hear what's going on, want to be included.

Two amplifiers will have to be built – one for desk use,
one that is self-contained and portable with its own batteries.
One will sit under my desk like an obedient dog,
and one I will lug around like a pet tortoise.

Sometimes I just want to fit in, blend into the background
like anybody else. But now I will have to pipe up.
All that bother, all that building, all those batteries,
if I'm as buttoned up as my winter coat, will be a waste.

I'll be a waste of time with my bulky attaché case.
Better perhaps to keep my ears shut, my mouth shut
and my ideas to myself. But I want this conference amplifier.
They tested me with an audiometer to measure my deafness.

I explained how I prefer my right ear to my left, how I sit
with people on my right if I can help it. Put my left ear
against the wall in the pub. Missing what's said over a pint is one thing –
missing an opportunity for a pay rise is another.

I like to hold a telephone receiver to my right ear. They told me
it's because it responds better to the higher speech frequencies.
Both my ears suffer from middle tone deafness, and I need
the maximum possible amplification. I know what that means.

It means I can't sit less than ten feet from the microphone.
They will have to save me a spot at the front. I will turn up
with my case of batteries and headgear receiver, the weight
of two newborns. It's 1938. Time to hear what's going on.

Ferocious
Selina Rodrigues

Dear Boss. Today your head is full of rain.
Your husband wept, you scraped plates at 3am

and still brought pastries. We watch. You are kind.
Children run the office in your eyes,

they run your heart with laughter. Imagine.
We are all hands to this juddering system.

Aire Street's window is open a hair's-width
enough for you, a thin, steady breath.

As sun sparks day, my wired head turns.
Lambs are eating, dying, calling. It's the season

you say. *Leave early because now the earth
is open-mouthed and fields are torn for birth.*

So hours pass through us until I trip
down tilting floors into ferocious spring -

- the city's form - feathered grey, slash, drop blue
contained new buds. Dear boss, away from you.

Rain falls again from untrustworthy skies.
I need the moors. For you, only commitment is right.

Daniella Has Good Lungs
Jacqueline Schaalje

Daniella told me she will skip Antarctica
because there are no trees there, only moss. But I like
soft moss, how until broken in by thaw it sucks
under the ice.

Don't you like moss? I asked Daniella. *I like to draw
the breath of forest around me*, she said. After the stifling
of moss, I thought of the mycelium of her young lungs.
Bubblegum pink.

Breathe all you want, I said. As long as breath
allowed I counted out how many new Adams and Eves
are born each second, drawn from the forest of their mum.
My bucket list:

The Congo Basin, Norway, Canada, Russia, good
places with wood. I mentioned the Amazon, at which we found
a few positive points to say about the company, too.
An arid place,

Eilat. No more than a clump of palm trees on the Red Sea.
Once, as I sat reading on a friend's balcony
a bee-eater alighted on top of my book. Its Zorro mask
and red bead eyes

hovered askance, but I wasn't going to show it our wet
markets. I'd rather it steered clear away. Since that fleeting
encounter I've switched to e-books, which birds don't get.
Catch out mistakes

breath by breath. Stark as night, bewildered and clawing,
trees lift us up and exchange us in breathing
which is their language. *How right you are to stand
and speak with them.*

Call
Christian Wethered

Once the reverse charge call was accepted
it was just you and your mother
light and distant
you could even hear her disquiet
in the miniature pauses
your father's rice cooking in the kitchen
the only way to reel her in
now she was caught unawares
was to pretend you were lonely
so she'd put down her spatula and clear her voice
and you'd know you had a few more minutes
while the crowd of boys outside your booth
faded and you were in her presence
could hear her breathe

Brothers
Theresa Muñoz

The writer Muriel Spark had an older brother, Phil. He existed like a forgotten tree.
He had no real impact on her work. In Martin Stannard's biography of Spark
Phil's big mention is on pages twenty to twenty two, brief as a twig crunch

in the fat dark. Nobody liked Phil. Spectacled and short, he flew box kites alone
to decompress from family bullshit. I have no brothers, only sisters.
Growing up I learned to eat fast, I learned empathy was all in the head tilt,

the sideways hum. Muriel Spark's brother had no real impact on her work,
those salty whodunnits. He liked typical boy things. He played by himself.
Phil liked to fashion wooden toys and crystal-set radios

he had the paper-gray drabness of permanent afternoons
he was ashamed of their Jewishness, their street like a ribbon
spooling down the hill. He did not feel pink rushes of love

from their parents, Bert and Cissy, who regularly polished Muriel's halo
and left him hanging in the side bar, his brows mulling
future departures. He wipes his glasses, eyes like sad triangles

and I think about brothers because I have none. I imagine one,
a brother with caramel skin and a wheel part in his hair like me.
Not sure where I'm going with this; maybe down a hall

into a hospital room, where a priest in aubergine tones
lay his hands on Dad's chest, still as a snowy town
Our brother Arturo, he kept saying, *Our brother we lay to rest*

but my dad didn't have brothers, he only had us,
that's why I think about brothers, their solid conveyance,
their ubiquitous presence; how they exist in all of us, like a dark barn.

The Actuaries
Emma Simon

We are beige fortune tellers, sifting patterns
in vast data sets. We watch the zeros swirl
and settle through our varifocals.

Sometimes we spot a cohort hidden
in the morbidity stats. Divining the divine
at work, we act accordingly: adjust their premiums.

We juggle probabilities, plot upward arcs,
cyclical trajectories. Try not to grab the flame
-lit end while conjuring alternate futures.

Forecasting is the art of necessary vagueness:
journeys and strangers, residual pension funds.
We map it all within our Delphic spreadsheets.

We wear thin smiles and worried suits,
stick to our own at office parties, the ones
who can fine-tune the metrics of disaster,

know it is never far away. Give us your palm.
We'll trace the lifeline through creases
in your genetic fingerprint. Predict when it will stop.

Sleep does not come easily. Not for us who count
the infinite dead instead of stars or sheep. Feel them
pressing close at night, like mispriced calculations.

Airline Miles
Michaela Coplen

I like to sit in the exit rows —
        and not, I admit, because I'll be of use if this goes
down. I like the exit aisle seat most
            (the exit row of the exit row) — those
floor lights underneath my foot, one elbow's

        free migration. Used to be I always chose
the window seats (for their windows) —
        I'd watch the city shrink until it almost
disappeared — all nestled in its nest of roads,
      the fields around in their own tight rows —

Now that oval shows me ghosts.
      How to leave a nation that claims you. *EXIT* glows
red overhead — I stretch my legs, I curl my toes.
      The tracking map is frozen. Time slows
over this ocean — it hurries going home. Homes,

      of course, are relative, like time's dividing zones;
I reckon the heart never really knows
      where it is, or else it can't disclose
its location except in cipher codes.
      I glance across — the window shows

no sign of what's ahead. Below's
      all that I've left — its known unknowns,
its aftermath, its overdose.
      Try and weigh your mother's oaths
against the debt that country owes.

      My hoard of airline miles grows.
When we land, I stand and coax
      my baggage down. We exit rows
and fill the aisle, clutching our coats,
      eyes meeting eyes — jet black, up close.

Hunting Season
Heidi Beck

A girl steps from a yellow bus
at Loon Pond Road, anticipating
a long walk home — down the hill,
around the pond, past the swamp
with the beaver dam, the final stretch
just woods — with her heavy bag of books.

It's hunting season, and the men
are out in pick-up trucks, stalking
through the woods with ammo, scopes
and shotguns, dressed in their camo,
carrying coolers stuffed with cans
of Budweiser, Coors, Tuborg Gold.

The girl puts on a safety vest, flimsy
fabric in fluorescent orange, begins
to sing — Supertramp, Fleetwood Mac,
all the lyrics to *Evita* — loud and long,
so they hear she is not a deer, so loud
she does not hear the pick-up truck slow

behind her. It pulls ahead, stops,
just past the swamp. *Hello, Honey,*
where you heading to? She smells
the beer as they corral her. *Let us help,*
all smiles and hands. The book bag drops,
the vest falls off, she's on her knees,

white rump to the air, trying to keep
her tail down. She shakes her head,
now fuzzy and furred, nose dark as dirt,
everything narrowed. Her ears stretch,
eyes widen, gaze becomes fixed,
the world slows. She remains still,

their laughter like an echo, then lifts
herself on spindly legs, fragile bones
at risk as she attempts to kick, hooves
flailing. She tries to buck and punch,
awkward in these limbs. Flanks damp,
she spins, all panting ribs, spins again, falls.

A girl steps out of the forest, arriving
for dinner, late. They glare at her clothes,
her hair, her wet, evasive face. She tries
to describe how she was a deer. *Stop!*
they cry, *stop with your lies, your make-
believe tales. Don't bring this trouble here.*

The girl with the light inside
Claire Dyer

packs the done day
into the brown leather case, slips
it beneath the bed into the space

where the dreams and darkness are.
Undressing, she removes
her face, switches off her light.

The night is always monstrous;
the static in her nightdress crackles
as she punctuates the hours

sitting upright like porcelain,
the deluge pooling the sheets as
moonshine leaks through

the half-drawn curtains
with the roses on, and when,
eventually, she sleeps she –

Instead of gulls
Sharon Black

I bring you jays and woodpeckers.
Instead of Mother's Pride white sand

and turquoise bars, here are
lavender, wild thyme and leggy sage.

In place of Columba's Bay:
this shrivelled stream, that sunken river.

I bring you bitten fingernails
and scabs across my knuckles

where a rock got in the way.
Also weeding, homework, soap suds,

dead mice, chicken shit,
a henhouse that needs cleaning.

I bring you questions, pleas, refusals, favours
and my mother-in-law's interruptions.

I bring you a paler version of myself.
I bring you eggs.

Mother's Mother
Alexandra Melville

Grandma slept with her eyes open,
making the walls and furniture disappear
through sheer willpower. Or as if
sight was a decision she stopped making.

Grandma believed tears were crocodile eggs
laid to snap at her ankles. *Watch yourself –*

she'd gasp, as though stung by salt.
Her veins were badly veiled under powder;
her skin broke on whatever it touched –

a satchel left in the hall, the leaf of a book.
You're so sharp you'll cut yourself.
I never thought of her as thin-skinned.

I dreamt a wild egg could take down
the swell of a cat's tit. A strange cure.

This is for those unwritten
lost by an open window, disappearing   behind blinds.

I was looking for you without trying
to see you –
                    even in the dark we avoided each other.

                    You spoke in half sentences and affronts.
                    Confronting mirrors, thinking about your mother,
                    your mother's mother.

You were peering into each room of your mother's house,
trying to go to sleep. Seeing again under closed lids
the marigolds from the kitchen window.

So much work year after year
and all the orange and yellow grief of it.

The roses staggering against the garage wall

verging on collapse.

Amicus Curiae Brief
Laura Davis

At last, I start to type, centred and bold,
"The case for legal personality
for Lake Victoria." I stop. Folders
of notes list everyday calamities –
industrial run-off, overfishing,
sewage – that destroy much aquatic life.
We could prevent this, keep the lake living,
as this particular legal device
confers additional rights, protects the lake.
Except: for proper standing in our laws
we must deny its true nature and make
a lake take human form and I am sure
that learning to respect it *as a lake*
will be the only way, for all our sakes.

Elegy to the howler monkeys
Maia Elsner

as their shrieks stab the heart of the undergrowth.
My cousin calls me *changita*, little monkey
& chucks me up, his branch arms sprawled, as I hang
upside down. I leap from tree to tree, his friends
welcoming me in. Sharp embrace. I am only fifteen
in the dark when you find me, toss me, fish & bait.

Later, in the C19th library, I read Fanny Hill. She is bait
for an old man. Walking back to my dorm, undergrowth
of nettles & thorns, no dock leaf: I am stung, fifteen
with paralysed calves, pulsating jugular. The monkeys
watch. Berger writes that women & women friends
are constructed to be seen, that we spectate ourselves. I hang

half-out of the window, wind through my hair. Hang
until I hear thumping. A boy sniggers & I take the bait –
start up something about feminism. My friend
says *the history of sex is only a very small undergrowth
of fully consensual encounters.* Usually one monkey
initiates & wants more & the other bears it. At fifteen

I probably don't say much or say it very well. Fifteen
is a time of miracles I don't remember. I hang
from the boat-sails of my sheets, my cotton monkey
climbing clouds. There's a pterodactyl on my wall, bait
for the meteorite I keep from wrecking. The undergrowth
keeps going. Watch the guava sky for sparks. My friends –

imaginary giraffe & ghost moth. The borders of friend-
ship are contrails of smoke. Puffy cheeks, I am fifteen
at the party. The bonfire burns into the undergrowth:
you were my friend & I trusted you, I hang
my syllables on sharp rocks, they break & I am bait,
ums & silences. Inevitably, I retreat to theory, monkey

at typewriter. Turn in my coursework. Play monkey
for grown-ups. Talk Marxism. Discuss with friends
the problems of university politics. I am bait
for a polite disagreement. But inside I am still fifteen
& I simmer, obsess over every touch. I am hung
up on detail, wade through the footnote undergrowth

of memory: bait the monkey, follow it to the edge
until the undergrowth thins & there's a clearing & friends
waiting for me. I am not fifteen. I hang my excuses.

How to talk to your children
Martyn Crucefix

When will we learn with the morning rush
to get ourselves our things out the door
compelled only by the pushy clock
not by boots in the street who might ask
who or what we are — by what authority
or by what right — instead this scrum
for books and shoes and mobile phones
and nothing proves easy to find
then it's hard to avoid the accusatory tone
(as this morning I sent you back
to scour bedside tables beneath clothes
behind each door in the cluttered dreck
of each brightening space)
O then it's hard to blame the behaviour
not the child — *you had it last night*
then dashed out back with your bag and now
you don't know where it is
so check the pockets of your coat again
and remember — listen — what I always say
how things get carelessly left
in the obvious place well don't they
so go check the pile on the dresser shelf
and *da! da!* the lost one waits patiently there —
just a moment before chaos resumes
our paused rush to the door
compelled only by the hands of this or that clock
(not by boots on the street who would
lean close would ask who or what we are
who are always quick to learn
how to exploit our predictable behaviours
whose powers depend on how alert we are
to the narrowing gulf
between life lived in jeopardy and life secure)

Madonna of the Parenting Manual
Fiona Larkin

Child, the challenge you present!
Where do I start with you, lamb of God?

A blue veil, drawn around my sallow
pallor, is humming with precise advice:

Let your behaviour always be objective
and kindly firm

for how else may I handle omnipotence
in your cherishable infant flesh,

and what to do with a good book
but follow it to the letter?

Never hug and kiss him
Never let him sit on your lap

Child, it is a preparation
and love is involved.

Hush: let me concentrate our angles
and perch you on my inner arm.

If you must, kiss him once
on the forehead when he says goodnight

I've kissed away a whiteness
on your rounded brow, with its hint

of widow's peak; and you raise a hand
to bless me, one among a multitude.

Shake hands with him in the morning

See how my fingers lengthen
with each ungiven caress,

and look at you, child, in your philosopher's
robe! Did you dress yourself?

Give him a pat on the head
if he has made an extraordinarily
good job of a difficult task

Little man, your proportions hide
the child I bore. Your hardest task

will see me break my faith
to hold you in the cradle of my arms.

Lines in italics taken from 'The Psychological Care of Infant and Child,' John B Watson, 1928

To husband
Tjawangwa Dema

> *Oh yes, I'm the great pretender –*
> The Platters

To husband
the way you thought you meant it,
I take a second job. Raise this boy
born with your face and none of its menace.
I chip at the door frame with eye and pen,
mark his spurts. Tell myself I will tell him,
when he's taller, that meaning comes
from time, its trembling intervention,
from being here. I'll tell him too, finally,
his father's body is alive somewhere.
That part-time Midas whose promises burnished
his small teeth and mine for a while.
I promise myself I'll practice before the mirror,
ready my face. Pray the words come
clean as brand new nappies.
I'll drive him here then, your son –
my love a pram –
point out your new wife. This house
with a roof that holds. Congratulations,
I heard she gave birth to a baby girl.
Baby, I've come to tell you
I've told our baby, you're lost
while I choo-choo'd pumpkin and broth
to his small, hungry mouth. Occupied
every cry, every creaking floorboard, every room
proclaiming his need. Now I say I don't know.
And I don't.
Not really.
The way you don't know his first word,
his best friend or the last thing he ate,

flat on his back with the slapped cheek.
Even gone you take up space.
Your absence means I can think only
of out-thinking this.
What to say when he asks.
When he asks, I point out the hellebores,
the quince and aconites.
I am finally the best at something,
a master at distraction. I dance my dance
before this constant looming
man-made hole in the shape of a father.
I say I don't know.
And I don't know you
not the way I've known the cost of formula
or the look of dawn after a sleepless night,
the feel of floor in that loud midwinter.
Not since you stopped pretending
I was laughing and gay
while you made-believe I was the clown.
You should know
when that little boy calls *mama*
I cast your ghost into the poorly-lit night
I say *let it follow your body,*
let it loom anywhere but here
as I fold his childish meaning into mine.

Breaking Waves
Helena Li

(1)

Tourist decked out in sunscreen
and a cheap roadside suit, chugging
Tsingtao and raw shrimp fresh from the ocean.

Charmed by shiny baubles along the sand,
I try somewhat successfully to forget
she was dying just hours away.

There is nothing more to say.

(2)

When waipo died, I missed the funeral to go to the beach.
Me slurping up blue shrimp along the shore
until my stomach is bursting with crawling things.

Tourist to loss, this is the only pain I can claim.

(3)

Eight years and the first time to see the grave
I poured libations from the shore.

Are you tired yet?

(4)

Before she dies, I lie next to her.
She has not eaten in days.
A few spoonfuls of broth.
No words between us.
Just her lucid brown eyes
peering out above the horizon
vast body of ocean
not afraid to drown in it.

(5)

I am trying not to forget her silences. *Forgive.*
I am not yet strong enough.

Wind-up Eyeballs

Paul Carney

So, draw him in your mind – the goatee beard; the knee-length shorts;
the backpack. Call him What-the-fuck's-his-name. Now – picture
me. My hair is red these days. With henna. Amber beads, and yeah,
I'm thinner. See – my jeans keep slipping down. So, for a day, my name
is Callipygia. We bump. His coffee spills. I laugh. His shirt
is wet. We're right outside a toy shop. We go in. It's called
spontaneity – look it up. He says the wind-up eyeballs have
blue irises – like mine. (My eyes are *sapphire*, actually.) I say
with dozy hipsters *chucking coffee everywhere, I need a few*
more eyes. He laughs. I'm funny. I can't help it. He says
something. Then we buy them. All the eyeballs in the shop. He's got
the money – but the thought is mine. We leave with two big bags
of eyes. So then we're squatting in the Asian style – easy for me,
I'm supple – on the pavement. So we turn the clockwork keys – and two
by two we set our eyeballs free. They're hopping. Clicking. Like
some kind of clicky hopping insect things – you'd know. We watch
small children pick them up. We watch black cabs
and buses crunching them to bits. So, me, I say *That's so*
like life. He tells me I'm *profound.* I am. So, tourists form
a laughing crowd. We stand. We take a bow. Applause. I hitch
my jeans back up. I'm holding one last eyeball. It's clicking –
vibrating in my hand. I hold it up in front of him – I stick it down
his neither-long-nor-shorts and say *I see you now.* He wants
my number – so I have to tell him: *There are too many of me*
for you to know. I blow two kisses over my shoulder. One
for him. One for the Council sweeping-man – he's brooming bits
of broken eyes along the gutter. Exit me.

advice from one who's been burnt before
Laura Theis

on the first day the dragon moves in
don't tell the neighbours but
take the batteries out of your smoke detector
you'll thank me later
you can stop paying your electricity bills
even asleep a dragon is more
than a room-full of candles

if you are stumped for what to feed your dragon
a little fire goes a long way
buy a multipack of tea lights
fire is what it breathes & what burns in its veins
it's also what it likes to snack on every once in a while
the way bees love to eat
honey but also make honey

oh and most important of all
if your dragon is thirsty give it verses but no water
never water but maybe a song if it is scared
stroke its wings till your hand scorches
or let it listen to the ember bloom rhythm of slow
soft breathing that rises from you like smoke
as you drift off in its glow

Entering her 50th year
Mel Pryor

She doesn't stop, as she eases herself down the river bank
in her bathing costume, mindful of deer shit
and roots and of the millions under her feet
       tunnelling into an underworld,
this woman – her smallness, her understanding
of her smallness – trusting the snug fit of mud and damp
grass under her foot soles,
       trusting that bare-toed she is safe from nick
and risk and gravel blade,

       out on one of her many early morning swims,
accustomed to the fish, unseen then seen from the bank,
the reeds, undulant, abundant below the surface
       on which a dragonfly's shadow hovers, its lechery
charmed into poise. Everything as it always is. No phone.
       No towel. No undressing.
She bends down at the river's edge to test the water,
immobile, apart from her moving hands,

attentive to the trees' modulations, the clean glaze of dawn
       laying itself down, and the leaves that gentle the surface
like an old communion touch. And it's already inside her,
her knowledge of the water's thirst for her body,
       of the clouds that people the river
as if they've arrived in reverse, thrown up from below,
those old ghosts that return with their waterlogged faces.
       Press on, press on, press on, they say.

On the far-side bank horse chestnuts
gallop east, willows unfold their drapery (keeping the houses,
       the road, even the distant pylon out of sight);
she steps in up to her knees, her thighs, navel, then steps deeper,
up to her ribs, up to her scar,

into the water, into her reflection,
and she lifts her feet from the river bed and swims,
the birds suddenly clamorous, and the river, endless,
endless the light down its back,
and the light hard, and clear.

The ringmaster's sleepless nights
Joolz Sparkes

Ladies and gentlemen, it's not the roar of the lioness
as she beds down with one of the lions that keeps me awake,

nor the smell of elephant dung mixed with straw or whiskey breath
from clowns filling my bunk, or tracks jolting the carriage

as we pass endless points, and although I could do without
bleary-eyed interrogations at borders trying to remember where we're

stopping next – Albania, Arkansas, somewhere beginning with A –
it's not this that bolts me upright at 3am or causes pitted black circles that

need to be pancaked over with greasepaint, nor the droop of moustache
that has to be perked up with black boot polish, no Madam!

It's not the constant worry of losing another bearded lady
to heart attack, nor bills mounting up, or caravan brawls,

or sequin stitching coming lose in the acrobat's hands,
nor the big top's battered and bruised patchwork quilt letting in rain.

It's not the arpeggio shrieks as the snakes get loose again or an emu
pecking my ear, or jugglers playing practical jokes with my shaving brush,

or the ambivalent looks from townsfolk wishing we were gone now they've
had their fun. It's not the family I left behind, the golden haired daughter

who'll never think of me kindly, that haunt my fitful nights - no Sir!
It's not the regret of forfeiting a pin stripe suit and the punching of a card,

nor the never tucking up all cosy at a fixed address. Boys and girls -
hear the ticking of the clock in my heart that punches

clean out of my chest like a balled fist and the tragic inner voice
that yells *why didn't you run away and join the circus sooner?*

Ladies and gentlemen, take a ringside seat and witness this idiot,
head in his hands with astounding regret at all those wasted years.

An afternoon
Pam Thompson

   where adult lads
up from Derby, in shirts and jeans
in January, ahead of the on-the-piss afternoon,
walk fast at the side of their reflections
in steel; the fountain near the station,
which, when the sun dips,
will spill onto the pavement and freeze.
In the Millennium Gallery,
Madonnas, flanked by fat putti,
vie for your attention
but you want something more subtle,
a painting or drawing that you'll
have to work at knowing.
Over there, on the other side,
with no-one else looking,
a watercolour under glass,
'Biography of a Snowdrop',
February 20th, 1896, its greyish flower
seeming too heavy for the stem –
how slowly she must have painted
while the light was still good.
Barely out of adolescence, its root,
scrotal, with white filaments.
For our convenience, she returned
on March 14th, prompted, perhaps,
by better weather, to draw exquisite
cross-sections of sex organs:
stigma and stamens; the segmented
flower like a star on a mosque
or a sliced fig, a tile, the day's tile.
Picking snowdrops first thing,
inside her own biography,
with spring lying in wait. Edith
Spiller. Look her up.

Khnum
Tabitha Hayward

And wouldn't you rather believe
a ram-faced god had settled to his wheel,
paid soft attention with his gentle hands,
moulding the silt and dirt, the river's bed, to form
this human child, still curled-up small
in the mud as in the womb, that sleek wet clay
hardening to outlines, red and grey
the colours of insides, our guts and flesh, the mess
of birth – but here, the artist knows his patient craft;
no rush of human error, passion, blood, but slow,
deliberate, kneaded into shape. Is all that care
a better kind of love? And wouldn't you rather believe
you are no accident, but meant to be – a god's
deliberate labour, worked for, achieved?

The Drone Studio
William Stephenson

I like to record white goods, especially freezers.
I fuss over them with microphones for hours.
Listen. That buzz is a domestic Electrolux
filtered through a nine-band graphic equalizer.
I've mixed it with the shriek of a Dyson on full power.
Can you hear the choir almost buried in the scream?
Those are cells singing; most dirt is cast-off hair and skin.

I'll play you my latest project. Cassette hiss
blended with the hum of a fading human brain.
Tranquil. I hear cliffs, a weathered coast, a shore
where tidal foam dissolves as it shrivels into sand.
Geese cry overhead, arrowing to warmer lands.
This donor's name was Simon. This sound's his legacy;
each cerebrum leaves a drone that's fingerprint unique.

So lie down, let me record you. I can upload the waveform
in loss-free format to the cloud. To enhance mindfulness
people listen on repeat. The feedback's been wonderful:
I weep as I play it in the car. Superb souvenir of my father.
Now close your eyes. Most see colours – blues, usually –
then nothing. As your heart slows, the colours darken.
Hear the last small wave the sea casts out before the calm.

This year
Rod Whitworth

I
When Omar Khayyam drew up his calendar based on his
calculation of how long it took the earth to orbit its star
he didn't know that, after nine centuries and one major change that
caused riots for lost days, we still would not have his accuracy.
You knew I was going to say that, didn't you?

II
When Omar Khayyam drew up his calendar
he didn't know he should have plotted that night in Amsterdam when
you knew and let me know.

III
When Omar Khayyam drew up his calendar, solved quadratics
and cubics, hinted at quintics
he didn't know that people would deny science in the name of his faith.
You knew that i was the square root of -1 and let me know in no
uncertain terms.

IV
When Omar Khayyam drew up his calendar and allowed ample
days for red wine, a book of verse and thou
he didn't know that you preferred white.
You knew though.

Distancing
David Butler

Now we are wintering - the whole hive stupefied
to silence, each in their cell who isn't soldiering,
an inmate of a new Shalott - the cities, simulacra:
drone-shot piazzas; enchanted palaces; empty
trainset trains; vistas dreamed by de Chirico;
traffic-lights sequencing the memory of traffic -
confined while, ineluctably, somewhere else,
the toll, the toll, until we're numbed by
the scale of it; each week, the heat and bustle
more distant, more unlikely; nothing to feed
but waxing apprehension: what will eclose
this long cocooning, and on what tentative wings?

lingua franca
Denisa Vítová

/ˌlɪŋgwə ˈfraŋkə/
noun
a language that is adopted
as a common language
between speakers
whose native languages
are different.
– Oxford Dictionary

Our lingua franca was love,
a pidgin, all broken up
in ungrammatical confessions,
semantic imperfections
we used to call inventions,
coining new words out of
white stains on satin,
lace on the bottom
of an overnight bag.

A home built on made-up letters
tongue-drawn inside a navel,
on strange idioms, neologisms,
verbs in rare positions:
on the brink of a sink
or pressed against the mirror,
no inflections
to hold onto.

Mapping each other,
a belly was a river,
a shoulder a mountain,
a back a landslide
to be buried into.
Renaming each other,

49

we struggled for power,
leaving traces on every mole:
who owns your name, owns you whole.

Our love was a colony,
mispronounced, misspelled,
displaced like a borrowed lexeme,
its meaning we didn't quite comprehend;
and all that time I only prayed
please God, forget me not,
rubbing my initials
over the ribs on your back.

Do we remember words
as single morphemes or whole forms?
It's not enough to not be forgotten,
it matters how you are recalled –
as the last syllable of a four-letter word
or a clitic standing on its own,
white stain on satin,
lace on the bottom
of a garbage bag.

This, darling,
is our language
death.

More Like Wrestling Than Dancing
Hannah-Lee Osborn

your space had been purged. I

recognized wanting in your
eyes. Fixed, I pictured
us comparing wrists
but my lips
were dry

and all the oceans home
were in my sight.

I'd wanted something else,
but this was how we said it

(goodbye).

Place Name: Bishan –
Rachel Lee

After Kei Miller

pronounced *bee-shun*, from the Mandarin 碧山, from the original
name 碧山亭, which points to a pavilion on a green mountain. I
could tell you it is green as in jade-green, in the ornamental stone
so treasured and worn. It was for nobility and immortality that
some buried their dead in suits of jade, and the lesser adorned
themselves with a bangle to the wrist, an inch-long cutout hung
around the neck. If you will, consider the word 'country' (国),
which is the word 'jade' (玉), surrounded by a wall of us who
protect the jade that protects us. So, when they begin to ship the
jade out on their own accord, perhaps the green becomes a sea-
green. As in the sloshing crests and troughs that spilled over my
ancestors on their way to this new shore. As in the colour their
faces turned when the teakwood junks bounced along the waves.
In time, this passed into Islam's paradise-green, greeting them
when they first found themselves moored to this feverish port-
town on the foot of the Malayan Peninsula. They would've seen a
forest-green, a moss-green of the tropical sort. Into this, they
gladly enfolded. Did Sir Thomas Stamford Bingley Raffles of the
British East India Company, when he later arrived, think how
lucky he was that that our wilderness did not bite back? That the
Singapore River is short and straight? That, in the intervening
years, no creeper of resentment then snaked around the native
heart? Here — let me paint you the better picture of colonialism
they'd hoped to see but couldn't ask for in review. A picture
wherein, a century and a half later, when the green beneath the
pavilions is trampled by the green of army fatigues under the
standard of the rising sun, we still believed that they would save
us. A diptych wherein a green poet writes and she writes in the
language of her coloniser, believing herself to be the master. A
triptypch wherein two centuries have passed and our institutions
hold fast to the copper-green glory of the Raffles name. But it is

none of these greens that is the green of Bishan, which is a softer, gentler green. This is the same green of the pasture in which my British lords' Lord will lead them to lie. And though there are, in truth, a want of mountains in this land, my people, too, dreamed of laying their kin to rest in lush fields of green.

The Line

Dipo Baruwa-Etti

My ability to create fiction oft causes friction between drama and reality.
I sometimes forget where I live.

> When I see an elderly woman walking with her daughter and they
> suddenly stop,
> I tell myself she's just died in her daughter's arms.
> Two minutes later, they take their next steps.

> When I see a black boy beside a white lady in church,
> I tell myself he's an orphaned foster child she has taken in.
> He's someone else's nephew.

> When I see you trying to smash down the barricaded door in anger,
> I tell myself your failure will cause you to burn the house down as
> we sleep tonight.
> You sweep it under the rug.

> When I see a man preparing to read the script without saying hello
> to me,
> I tell myself after this is done he will call me a nigger.
> A lovely greeting is exchanged.

> When I see my neighbour being wheeled into an ambulance,
> I tell myself he's been cursed by a witch and will die.
> Yet to return, I continue to weave the web.

High stakes are oxygen to a story's existence.
Protagonists are expected to trawl through dirt, falling deeply
into despair.

This muddles my days.

And One Day It Stopped
Nathan Evans

just stopped   dead   on beaches
rocks   kids were first to notice
dropped spades   buckets   pointed
look Mummy   Daddy   the sea
stopped breathing   parents exchanged
glances   *damn*   they should've
got around to signing that petition
taken out the recycling   fishermen
noticed next   boats ground
to standstill   nets wouldn't fill
damn   they shouldn't have petitioned
for an increased allocation   then came
reporters   with exclamation marks
and wide-shots of water one might walk on
to the mainland   all along the coastline
crowds gathered   swooshed fingers
of encouragement in the ocean's hem
come on   but it wasn't playing
sleeping sealions   no prizes would be won

Ode in the wrong time and place
Sarah Barnsley

O stupid Grief, you're in the way – I was busy
writing a love poem until you barged in, your big
bag stuffed with crisps and gum to keep you going
on your ciggie run to Ostend. Look at what your
ticket says, it stipulates that you belong to 1965,
with 'the girls', escaping *your* mum, and *my* poem
is the one with great white cliffs in it, no *please* don't
turn it into Dover or wherever it was your boat departed
from, *these* cliffs are supposed to be safe and stacked
in Sussex where my heart is and grown today as big as
the Downs and keeping going like G and I did walking
that fine day in April. O Grief you are not meant to be
here, I implore you *not* to take me off my feet, get back
to your ferry, see those Belgian illuminations you loved
so much and let the sun on a perfect spring day continue
to light up our faces, quick, before it gets dark.

Goldfinches
Mark Fiddes

Our tea cools down, the last from the pot.
Through the kitchen window we watch
two goldfinches pecking seed from a feeder.
Old storm clouds smoke along the tree line.
Everywhere else has floods, as firemen
rescue an incontinent island from itself.
They say another superbug is on its way.
Leather or rust has seeped into the room.
I can't see him
when he asks how he's done as a father.
I tell him
I haven't found the job description yet.
It's not the answer we are looking for
because we learned to tie our bow loose
enough to bind, not to pull on the rope.
Unlike mothers whose knots tighten on
the spring tide and motions of the moon.
Instead, we riff on goldfinches.
How they mistake England for paradise.
How winter crushes them
from melodious primroses.

Waste: A History
Jo Brandon

We'll never really know what was crossed
with what, our best guess is *Dionaea muscipula,*
more commonly known as *Venus Flytrap,* turned
polytypic by splitting and re-seeding strands
of *Sundew* and *Bladderwort,* all of one genus,
more or less, quite natural, they surmised,
to combine them. Add a little bioengineering here,
a little bionic support there, resulting in
the volume capacity of a city rubbish truck.
All waste fed through jaws that looked no bigger
than the average man's head, but expandable
to the size of the, oft cited, beach ball
(*circa* 1991A.D.). Nature's safety-catch,
in the form of the two stimuli trigger hair,
was considered unnecessary. It is fair to conclude,
without much specific citation, that this was
one of their primary errors in judgement.
They enhanced the plant's ability to form
a hermetic seal and digest whatever
it consumed, perfect to dispose
of all that waste, no need to reduce,
only to feed. Adapted it to self-propagate,
like garden-variety poppies, wherever refuse
was most pervasive, sowed a little AI
so the *Purgamentorum Comedenti* could
itself discern between refuse and other.
It did so with organic abandon.
Once the statistics became dire
Homo Sapiens had to disguise their true nature.
Needed to cross-breed and reseed to escape
the crushing judgement of the *Waste Eater.*
Characteristically they could have chosen *Ivy* or
Lesser Bindweed but it would have been unscientific

to proceed on such a basis; they looked instead to the Ancients, remembered Daphne's escape from the cruel embrace of Apollo and took on the limbs of a *Laurel*. No name for this species survives. That too was an error in judgement.

Tidal Race
Kathryn Bevis

This morning found you capsized
and sinking in the campsite kitchen,
bloodless, clammy, haunted by the world
and all its doubles. They hauled you off
in their blue-light bus and I rode
beside, squeezed your shoulder tight,
and willed you back to yesterday.

Drowning here, the reflected twin
of everything swims in your eyes
and pulls you far from reach. They wheel
you out and in, from scan to scan,
pump dye around your veins
and brain to find the chink
that let the shadows seep inside.

Hours slide behind
this green curtain and still
you get your sums wrong, still
believe in clones of fingers, faces, clocks
that press at the corners of your eyes,
maintaining they exist, insisting
on their right to be here.

Come back. We'll grip the cliff edge
while the seal's sleek head lifts
above the water's surface, melts
to gloss again. Gannets will plunge,
gold-hooded, into the tidal race
and splash to scoop out cloud-marked
mackerel, flaring silver in the sun.

to my brother's ex-wife whom I saw on the northern line
Arji Manuelpillai

I thought I would f' and blind
truncheon-stare, all gritted teeth,
all rage inside the tube
so you'd recoil as if eating

shit by accident, I wanted you
to know how he'd stumbled
the wet streets bottle-handed
smash, squeezed the shards

till juice flowed from his fist.
I found him staring at his knees
like they weren't his own, crying
as he had when I pushed him

from the top bunk so his thumb
cracked back, I wanted you to
know we drove to Brighton,
it was all I could think of to do

to show him I loved him, that it
would be ok, that I would kill you
a thousand times if he told me to
I wanted to say you were forgotten,

that in Brighton we made a den
from cigs and beer bottles, kissed
temples as a fire blazed and
he laughed at you, screaming,

scorched beautiful and mama
rang me, said she was worried.
I gripped the back of his neck.
We never made it to Brighton,

I couldn't find the tenderness
the angle to hold him, ended
up at home, eating biriyani,
telling my mum how much we loved her.

Photograph of Joe Strummer as a Gravedigger, St Woolo's Cemetery, Newport, 1974
Jonathan Edwards

This is the pause before his life begins.
Here, there is no crowd of screaming fans,
no skin-clad groupies waiting in the wings,
and what applause there is is just the wind.
These are the years of bedsits, hand-to-mouth

and this: you put your hobnailed boot to it,
your knackered back to it, you turn the earth,
the world, you tuck the dead up, tuck them in.
These are the years before he's anything:
his post-work snack is not a mountain range

of powder and his donkey jacket's not
a fashion statement. These are the years he is
anyone and in this photo here
he looks into the camera and his eyes
know nothing of all *that* in front of him.

These are the years. The day is blinking cold
and still there's something here you don't quite know
a way to say it. Look. His grin. Or how
he holds himself. That shovel standing there,
like any second now he'll pick it up

and play it.

Our Household Goods
Andrew George

The first few days we sat here all alone,
dull as water in this kitchen sink,
then you recalled manhandling the TV
into the house, some pulley system you'd
dreamed up, a job I'd thought impossible,
a lad from Dixons stood outside and gawped,
and so I spoke of how you sourced this couch,
sorry, this chaise-longue, from central Wales
and how we rolled and lugged it into place -
an old design originally from Norfolk
copied by two men in Llanidloes,
and sadly stained that night your college friend,
before he moved to Frankfurt, slipped and spilled
his vintage port, the bottle that we won
at our church fête or maybe the school raffle,
he didn't catch the curtains though, pre-dating
us and chosen by that New York shrink
from whom we bought the place, though maybe he
inherited them too from the man
who went to jail for fraud, thrown in with
the house by his bankruptcy trustee,
I rather like their clashing pastel shades,
the rope we pulled to draw them on the day
we brought our baby home and laid her in
the cot she soon outgrew, we swapped it with
this sofa-bed for when your mother stays,
ergonomically designed in Sweden,
finished by machinists in Taiwan,
which made us feel we're locked down here together,
not just us, but also all of them.

Cargo Cult

Adam Lowe

They strapped me down and wedged wood
between my teeth. Their potions sat on my chest,
a lead-heavy beast: a succubus sipping at my lips.

They nailed their order over my bed, a decree
not to trust, listen or free me. I was a witch,
a traitor and liar. I didn't know my own flesh.

With incantations of their own, they denounced
Pazuzu, Baphomet, Lilith and Ba'al Hammon.
They made me a crucible for their cargo cult.

They called on their gods: conversion therapy
and *Living Marxism*; they distorted Engels and Marks,
called their whispers CBT. But their devotion was sorcery.

I was racked and poisoned, berated and disbelieved.
I howled vengeance at the moon, attempted
my own summoning: calling Aiwass, Quetzalcoatl and Kali.

Lift me on duppy strings, I screamed, and free me
from this bed! I begged Lakshmi and Huracan for release;
I scorned Artemis, Venus, Horus instead.

I sang a plea to Serapis, spat at Jupiter.
I defied the wrath of Yahweh and Zeus.
Still they kept me down, chained and gagged.

At last, I burnt to holy flames, licked high
to touch the ceiling. In agony, I breathed
and toasted them all in my rage.

Isaac Marks was the author of 'Treatment of Sexual Deviations:
Electric Aversion Therapy of Sexual Deviations'.

Rain
Vanessa Lampert

Rain you knew was coming
because the *will it rain today* app
said you could bank on it. Rain
that falls so hard the drains
can't cope. Rain that's silver
and says *right now this road
is my river* then gets down
and does it. Rain that quickens
then quietens. Rain that answers
the questions grass asks. Rain
that explains gravity. Rain
that repeats this again and again
like a patient teacher. Rain
that pleases birds. Just listen
to them. Rain that is torrential,
relentless. Rain that is only
tiny aerosol droplets, the kind
of light rain that makes you
really wet. Rain that fucks
the day over by not letting up.
Rain that's unexpectedly warm
when you're swimming in
the cold sea knowing for once
you've outwitted it so you
tell this to the sky. Rain
that comes on your birthday
every year and what did you
expect, boy born of a Scottish
autumn? Rain that doesn't
touch us because we're indoors,
listening to its quiet music
of fall, not saying much at all,
and you stayed, and you stay.

The sex training-video is full of plot holes/socks
Katie Griffiths

After Will Gompertz's review of 'Fleishman Is In Trouble'
by Taffy Brodesser-Akner

Maybe I'm missing something.
Maybe that's how folk are
in New York.

Most of the 26 minutes are padding
and the cerebral side doesn't get
a shoe in.

Sex is a braggart
with cufflinks
and a convertible

who whips out
diagrams.
(Arrows. Ellipses. Bull's-eyes.)

Marriage is a slugger
with saucepans
and a dialect

who's ditched the job
in a smoke-charred diner
to train as a nurse on an industrial site.

Why don't you take your socks off – *and let the air get to your feet, dear?*
Seriously –
this level of unsolicited advice.

Why don't you take your socks off – *and let your convertible get to the air.*
Why don't you take your socks off – *and let New York get to your convertible.*
Why don't you take your socks off – *and let your marriage get to New York.*
Why don't you take your socks off – *and let the cufflinks get to your marriage.*
Why don't you take your socks off – *and let the nurse get to the cufflinks.*
Why don't you take your socks off – *and let the air get to the nurse?*

Skywards
Jonathan Greenhause

The sky is full of our words. We speak them,
& out they flow, upwards,
diagonally, not quite parabolic.
They float there, buoyed
by some unspoken gravity. Our syllables
hookworms seizing the firmament,
wet clothes swaying
upon a clothesline, our syntactic wisdom
burnt piecemeal by the sun, our foolishness
swirling hurricanes, twisting
into tornadoes. Our manifestoes
get sucked into jet engines,
cause them to crash into the oceans
too waterlogged for our wishes,
too fond of drowning sound. We release
a swarm of butterflies en masse,
accessorize their wings
with adhesive tape, seek to recapture
our slant rhymes, our bro-
ken lines, our metaphoric rise. Our language
becomes defined as ungrounded
as we air out our grievances, as we build
a literal foundation in the atmosphere,
breathe out conjunctions
& but rather than whether if though
to link them with our lost words, latch them
onto adjectives, beg them
to skip back home. We're thrown
into silence, are left with a list
of countries whose muted citizens
can no longer express
the connections that kept us from soaring off.

A Violet I Plucked from Mother's Grave*
Elizabeth Neal

In memory of Mary Jane Kelly 1863-1888

I have been in many places
before I arrived here –
I have been a daughter, scholar, wife,
a widow and picker of wild flowers –
see *this small violet*
I plucked from Mother's grave.
I have been a brunette, redhead,
a blonde with blue eyes.
I have been a pleaser of men,
a drinker of gin
and singer of songs
of mothers, babies and of *this small violet*
I plucked from Mother's grave.
I have slept in many beds,
been a dweller of slums,
a breaker of windows,
an inmate of cells
and an owner of debt
but while life does remain
I'll keep singing and retain
this small violet
I plucked from Mother's grave.
I have been a mutilated corpse,
an object of speculation
and a media star.
I have been dead,
I have been alive –
all these things I have been
but while life does remain,
I'll keep singing and retain
this small violet
I plucked from Mother's grave.

*The song Mary Jane Kelly was singing on the night she was murdered

In Regent's Park
Kathy Pimlott

Then I thought I heard a lion's roar, a command
to surrender. But all I could see was cow parsley
lapping the legs of silver birches, an ice house
overtaken by ivy. All flights grounded, birdsong
was flooding the quiet – chinking, fluid, making
a deep summer of April. A green woodpecker
laughed from above. I couldn't see him but knew
he was there. Hemmed in, fancy seeks out crevices
which give onto savannah. It's not unreasonable
to think I heard a lion, or perhaps it was a tiger.

People came
Nicky Kippax

and went, brought umbrellas to dribble across the floors of our house, as if everything wasn't sodden enough already. We spent hour-minutes wringing out rugs and blankets with swollen fingertips. Soups and casseroles that would never be eaten boiled ludicrously on the stove while our children sloshed over to the door, small hands on small hips, to announce the bad news - freshly - for each arriving visitor. Later, they would crawl around, noses to tideline, imitating what they thought a heart attack might look like. Little bodies pulsing and fretting on the carpet. They began to cause nervous laughter and I didn't know how to put a stop to that with tender words, so I distracted them with a life-raft in the shape of a dinosaur, which they idly pushed around. In fact, we didn't talk much at all that day because of the weight of the water but we certainly managed to fool ourselves. Moving around like ordinary people, ordinarily clothed and with ordinary Sunday plans, even as the water rose by three feet, then four. It turned grey-green, stiffened with salt and lipids - and as the rooms grew late-October dark, I realised that we could only see the whites of everyone's eyes. No-one thought to switch a light on so we just continued lurching about in the soggy mess. Someone thankfully burned themselves on a pan which had sizzled white-dry and the ensuing study of scalded flesh became our point nemo for a welcome minute-hour. We spent a disproportionate amount of that time touching and dressing the wound, asking about the quality and originality of pain it caused. By the time night came, bubbles were escaping from the corners of our mouths, so children were bundled into clammy beds and everyone else waded home to their own private skitter of dreams. We, remaining, finally turned on a lamp to see us through until dawn and held each other hard - dry but spangled warrior-lovers with bodies like a wreck of flightless birds, listening out for the slow scintilla of a new day to mark this moment. The end of a first night without you.

LIVE CANON